LOUIS XIV AND THE FLOWER GIRL OF THE ORANGERY

A Comedy–Vaudeville in one act

LOUIS XIV AND THE FLOWER GIRL OF THE ORANGERY

A Comedy−Vaudeville in one act

DE VILLENEUVE AND MASSON

Translated and Adapted by Frank J. Morlock

WILDSIDE PRESS

CHARACTERS

LOUIS XIV
THE MARQUISE DE MONTESPAN
THE PRINCE DE MARSILLAC, the confidant of the King
THE DUKE DE SAINT–AIGNAN, Captain of Guards
DESMARETS, Controller General of Finances
GRAIN–D'ORGE, rich cattle merchant
PERETTE, A Gardener attached to the Orangery
GUILLAUME, Master Gardener
MACLOU, Gardener lad
Gentlemen, Gardeners, etc.

DEDICATION

This play is dedicated to the memory of Bill Pearlman, actor, author, playwright, poet, mentor and good friend. It was good knowing you, and I wish I'd known you better.

ACT I

The action takes place at Versailles.

The stage represents a section of the Park at Versailles, near the Orangery; in the middle a statue of Louis XIV.

Gardeners are working. One is atop a tall double ladder; the others are busy trimming and the others are picking up the trimmings

CHORUS

Come on, Come on,
Work with care,
Trim, gnaw, cut,
But especially manage
The flowers and the buds.

GUILLAUME (entering)

When duty calls us
It's not like at the court,
For each in his turn
Gets to the top of the ladder!

CHORUS

Come on, come on,
Work with care,
Trim, gnaw, cut,
But especially manage
The flowers and the buds.

GUILLAUME

Well! the rest of you haven't finished yet. Still, you know that for some time now His Majesty Louis XIV often comes to stroll near the Orangery here in Versailles—you cannot be here when the lords arrive,—nobles like that wouldn't like to find themselves face to face with villains like you.

FIRST GARDEDNER BOY

Suffice, master Guillaume—there I'm 'bout done—all I got left to do is pick up the flowers.

GUILLAUME

In that case, you can leave right away, 'cause there's somebody else tasked with that duty. It's my little cousin Perette who I had sent from Normandy exactly for that.

FIRST GARDEDNER BOY

All the same she's a comer, your cousin—she's a fine slip of a girl— a morsel fit for a king, that—

GUILLAUME

In that case she's none of your business. As for you, Mr. Maclou, exactly, there she is coming this way with her little ole basket. Do me the pleasure of taking your basket and going to work further off.

CHORUS

Come on, come on,
Work with care,
Trim, gnaw, cut,
But especially manage
The flowers and the buds.

(They leave.)

(Enter Perette carrying two baskets which she sets down.)

PERETTE

Let's set to work quickly.
My two baskets should have already been filled.
I slept too late, it's a shame.
But I was dreaming of the country:
I thought I saw my village clock,
Heard my dog barking at my flock.
I speak the language of our peasants
And I repeated the village lingo.
Tra, la, la.
I still think of the country,
But every day
My heart tells me
It's better here at court.

Innocent games are customary.
No one really loses, I think
For a wager you have to kiss
The sweetest girl: that's me!
The tambourine, the sound of the bag pipe,
They're already calling us from a distance to the elm.

Every lad invites a young filly
To dance the village dance, I bet.

> *(dancing)*

Tra, la, la.
I still think of the country,
But every day
My heart tells me
It's better here at court.

GUILLAUME

It's very nice of you to sing to me like that, my little Perette—but that doesn't change the fact that for more than an hour these flowers really need to be picked up.

PERETTE

I was going to tell you, cousin, that just now I again met a gentleman who kissed me and who delayed me.

GUILLAUME

Bah! he kissed you?

PERETTE

Yes—but he's old—you know very well he's the one called the Superintendent of His Majesty's Gardens.

GUILLAUME

Mr. LeNotre—oh! him—that's different, seeing that he kisses the King when he wants to——They even say that when he was in Rome he kissed our Holy Father the Pope.

PERETTE

To no one else would I have permitted it. Really, not even you, cousin, Guillaume.

GUILLAUME

With me—it's good friendship, but with others, that could become dangerous.

PERETTE

Oh! I know that well enough—my father told me that a week ago when I left the country. Down there, be careful, Perette.— With that, it's to save me from a similar danger that I was sent to you.

GUILLAUME

Bah! you haven't spoken to me yet about that.

PERETTE

Well yes! you remember quite well Mr. Grain-d'Orge, that rich cattle merchant from the neighboring town,—all the time he spent at our place. He used to stop at our farm—and he spent every day there.

GUILLAUME

What! did that Mr. Grain-d'Orge speak to you of love? A man who has millions!

PERETTE

No question, he told me I was pretty, that he wanted to be my type— he talked of giving me presents—do I know-

(Singing)

He spoke to me of his riches;
He boasted of his good humor;
He swore to adore me forever;
He constantly talked of my happiness.

GUILLAUME (singing)

Yeah, but—now, to make a nice household,
They say all you need is a husband.

PERETTE

Something still was lacking.

GUILLAUME (singing)

What was that?

PERETTE

Any talk of marriage.

GUILLAUME

I'm no longer surprised, then, that your father sent you to be with me. You couldn't hope to be the wife of a man so opulent—who is a noble now—a baron!

PERETTE

Still it's true—as they say in the country, that it's a favor from the court—that cost him a thousand crowns!

GUILLAUME

Believe me—forget about it.

PERETTE

Oh! I've already forgotten him, I am so comfortable here—you are so good to me. You see so many beautiful things.

GUILLAUME

Eh! well yes, child—but the thing is, that you sometimes neglect your work. You don't go in every alley of the Orangery, you're always around here, where there often isn't a flower to pick—while on the other side, the earth's seeded with them—and if your service were complained of—it might get to the ears of the king.

PERETTE

That's true and I don't wish to vex him, 'cause if my father possesses a small farm with four acres of land, he owes it to him.

GUILLAUME

Yes, that day His Majesty was hunting, the King fired on a stag and your father got the ball in his leg. That was lucky. Well, he made his path with that broken leg—now that's what caused his fortune.

PERETTE

Eh, to say that he doesn't recognize me, this great King, and I no longer have the honor of seeing him.

GUILLAUME

Well, right here, there's his statue, look at it completely at your ease.

PERETTE

Oh, I recognized it already.

GUILLAUME

Do good work and come rejoin me when you've finished, bye, my little Perette.

(Guillaume kisses Perette on her face and leaves.)

PERETTE

Bye, Cousin, Guillaume.

(she sets to work picking up flowers)

Oh, yes—I really know it, that statue. I've already looked at it enough for that. Heck, it's quite natural, the benefactor of my family. I spend whole hours in front of it, and then I scold myself. Well, it's all the same, I always come back despite myself. Oh, but—I don't want to be caught at it any more—like yesterday—by that great lord who asked me my name, my age, for goodness sake! He really promised me that next Sunday, at Chapel, he'd seat me in such a way as to see His Majesty, then I could really see the King.

(singing)

At church, I hope
To gawk at him at leisure.
His grandeur, his magnificence,
Ah! how it all dazzles me.
I'd be scared to be in his presence,
But I'd shiver with so much pleasure.
Yes, I'd be scared to be around him,
But I'd shiver with so much pleasure, anyway. (repeat)
I bet he's going to notice me.
My God! Look how I'm blushing already
He hasn't yet told me I am pretty,
How nice it would be for a king to tell you that!
At church I hope
To gawk at him at leisure.
His grandeur, his magnificence,
Ah! how it all dazzles me!

(stopping before his statue)

I always come to contemplate his image.
Ah! how many tears this fear must cost me,
But, at least I'm sure of remaining a good girl.

*(she remains lost in admiration of the statue without
noticing that an orange flower is falling out of her basket)*

Well, I spilled all my flowers.

(she picks them up in a hurry)

At church I hope
To gawk at him at leisure.
His grandeur, his magnificence,
Ah! how it all dazzles me!

(speaking)

Clumsy that I am, I never do it with others. If I was seen? Right, see everybody's coming. It's over, next time I come here I won't look at the statue any more. Absolutely. If I can prevent myself.

*(Perette continues to pick up her flowers and
then disappears without being seen by Marsillac
and the other gentlemen who enter.)*

MARSILLAC (laughing as he enters)

Ah! ah! ah! by Jove! Gentlemen, this is going to cause a great scandal at court.

DESMARETS

What's the matter, Prince de Marsillac? I arrived just as it was being explained: I don't know the topic under discussion.

MARSILLAC

My word, Milord Controller General of Finances, the thing is that his Majesty just received a deluge—

DESMARETS

The King?

MARSILLAC

The King! And the funniest thing is that his royalty was precisely the cause of the trouble—two gentlemen of the first rank were arguing over the honor of presenting him a cloak which he finally received from a valet.

DESMARETS

Well—I don't see anything extraordinary in that—just that Louis XIV wanted to avoid getting wet.

MARSILLAC

What, you don't understand that it's a total reversal in the King's service? Etiquette.

(sings)

It's on that that depends, I trust,
The safety of the monarchy.
At the court of a great king
Nobility takes place before patriotism.

Let our soldiers starve;
Let them experience a defeat
For us—who cares—for after all,
The people may lack bread
But the Court must protect etiquette.

DESMARETS

But I perceive Madame the Marquise de Montespan is coming here with the Duke de Saint Aignan.

(All greet the Marquise as she enters.)

MADAME DE MONTESPAN (after having made a deep bow)

Gentlemen, we are preceding the King by a few moments—we left him with LeNotre who is explaining to him his new ideas on the double stairs.

MARSILLAC

His Majesty won't be slow to join us, I am sure of it—because the Marquise is already with us.

MADAME DE MONTESPAN

You always flatter me, prince; that makes me believe what they say at court—that you are not of my friends.

MARSILLAC

Ah!—Marquise, aren't you the best friend of the King—

MADAME DE MONTESPAN

That's true; up to now I've known how to deserve the kindnesses of Louis—and so long as the heart of the King belongs to me I can count on the attachment of his court. But here's Mr. Desmarets.

(she bows to him)

I am enchanted to see you. They've assured me that yesterday, Mignard displayed, in your presence and before all these ladies, this portrait of the King that he's just finishing—they say it's admirable.

SAINT-AIGNAN (low to Marquise)

I get it—Madame the Marquise understood that this precious image ought to come to her one day.

MADAME DE MONTESPAN

Hush! Much lower in front of them!

(aloud)

Well, what does the Comptroller General think of this new masterpiece?

DESMARETS

My word, Marquise, seeing the image of the King, my master, I thought only one thing—it's that the coffers of the Treasury are empty, that all the services are in need and that the people—

MARSILLAC

What's that? the people! My dear Comptroller—what ideas! When the court demands it of you, first off, you must pay—as to the rest, create the resources, that's your job.

(sings)

When the people experience a misfortune,
Reassure them with words,
If they cry out, so that they'll shut up,
If taxes are demanded:
In the end, overwhelm them with taxes;
Then gold will abound in the coffers.
Pay them with their own money,
Then all is well with the world,
And the people are always happy.

(speaking)

Wait, listen to a plan I've conceived. Make money out of the nobility.

(Marsillac takes Desmarets by the arm and walks with him to the back of the Orangery; the other gentlemen stroll about and appear to talk confidentially as Madame de Montespan leads the Duke of Saint–Aignan forward.)

MADAME DE MONTESPAN

Now, my dear Duke, we are alone, answer quickly the question I was addressing to you as you entered. Shouldn't you deliver to me that letter that LaValliere addressed to the King?

SAINT-AIGNAN

I intercepted it—here it is.

MADAME DE MONTESPAN

Fine—I will read it. She's renouncing the world. The King can do no more for her—I'm doing this so the King will not be pained.

SAINT-AIGNAN

You are so good! and besides, what could you fear from this old passion?

MADAME DE MONTESPAN

Perhaps I was wrong to alarm myself—and yet, why this coldness by the King for some days? Why did he come twice to walk mysteriously in this part of the Orangery, solely accompanied by that flatterer Marsillac, who you know, is the secret confidant of the King's intrigues? I must suspect it's again a question of a concealed love intrigue.

MARSILLAC

Gentlemen, here's the King.

SAINT-AIGNAN

Silence! they're coming.

> *(Everyone forms up at the arrival
> of the King and his suite.)*

CHORUS

Here's the King; on his way
To his grandeur, (repeat) let's render homage.
Here's the King (repeat)
Respect, love, for us that's the law.

KING

Very fine, gentlemen, I admire your devotion to my person.
For a few drops of water, you all left me.

MARSILLAC

His Majesty can suppose that near him, the rain of Versailles doesn't dampen.

KING

No, but it gives you a bad cold and I noticed it during the argument between Mr. de Tresmes and de La Rochenfoucauld. I beg you, gentlemen, that such things never happen again. Etiquette must be respected. But not to satisfy the pride of some servants. Henceforth, gentlemen will be excused from accompanying me in my morning strolls.

MADAME DE MONTESPAN

Still, the honor of following Your Majesty each day excites the ambition of his court—and especially mine.

KING

Yes, Marquise—but as for me. I want to escape from time to time from the atmosphere of intrigues that so often surround me. I am the King of France and not the prisoner of the court. I intend to be free to go where I like, to receive who I like. Yesterday, gentlemen, If I'd listened to you, I wouldn't have admitted Moliere to my table. That will force you, I hope, to receive him at yours. If you were to have among you a man of genius, the monarchy, won't be worse off for that—

DESMARETS (aside)

It wouldn't be better off for it.

KING

Moreover, my pleasures are dear to me and besides, they are necessary to the renown of my royalty. You will continue to present yourselves for my trips to Marly, but mornings, only Marsillac will accompany me this week.

MARSILLAC

Your Majesty overwhelms me with honor.

MADAME DE MONTESPAN(low to Saint–Aignan)

I told you so—they're on guard against us—but we will thwart the intrigue.

DESMARETS

Will I be allowed to ask a moment's audience with Your Majesty?

KING

Ah! it's you Controller General. I'm sure of it; yet more complaints to address to me.

DESMARETS

It's not I, Sire, it's the people who are complaining.

KING

And what are they complaining of?

DESMARETS

The tax of the tenth, that I want Your Majesty to adopt.

KING

Your plan of imposing a tenth has given birth in me to religious scruples— I've submitted it to the Sorbonne, I am awaiting its response.

DESMARETS

But, Sire, next month—

KING

First of all let's think carefully of foregoing it. You cannot double the capitation.

DESMARETS

It was tripled last year.

KING

I've created thousands of charges and offices. Don't you also have letters of nobility? There's a revenue for the Chancellery.

DESMARETS

They are now in really great discredit. It's reached the point that it's necessary to employ force to have accepted those that Your Majesty deigns to grant.

KING

And what's it matter—so long as they pay?

DESMARETS

But, they are refusing to pay. Just yesterday I received a very uncivil latter from a cattle merchant from Normandy, the rich Grain-d'Orge.

(sings)

He won't listen to anything on the subject.
All my efforts are useless.
And to the title of Baron I would grant him
At the lowest price— Sire, a hundred thousand crowns!

KING

My dear chap, come to an agreement with this man
And name him, if he's very demanding,
Count or Marquis, for his money.
But make sure to get the money.

(speaking)

But—don't come to complain endlessly. What the devil, the affairs of the people are not my business, they're theirs. I've really enough to occupy myself with the etiquette of my Court—the works of Versailles, the interests of my family.

MARSILLAC

Indeed, Milord Comptroller, His Majesty has grave occupations at the moment.

(low to the King)

Sire, I think I observed that little one who comes here.

KING

I hope she doesn't know you noticed her trouble, her agitation, when she is in front of this statue.

MARSILLAC

Far from it, Sire, yesterday, when questioning her, I didn't even let her guess who I was.

KING

(aloud to his suite)

Gentlemen, accompany the Marquise into the park. Consult Le-Notre's plans for the fountain of Latona and the baths of Apollo. I will go rejoin you. Marquise, I await your approval.

MADAME DE MONTESPAN (making a curtsy)

Sire, that's too great a favor.

(low to Saint–Aignan)

We must obey—

KING (to Marsillac)

Accompany her.

CHORUS

Let's leave the king, according to custom,
To leave him (repeat), he directs us
Let's leave the king. (repeat)
Respect, love, that's our law!

> *(Marsillac affectedly offers his hand to
> Madame de Montespan, who affectedly replies.
> They leave followed by all the others.)*

KING (alone)

I see her coming. She's got her basket. Ah! if she's only coming to pick flowers from these orange trees, if she doesn't stop at the statue, the charm will be destroyed.

> *(he hides behind one of the orange trees)*

From here I can see her at my ease.

PERETTE (entering)

Well, but, now what am I doing? I don't have any business here. What, here I am again—luckily, my cousin Guillaume went on an errand in Versailles.

KING (aside)

She is charming.

PERETTE

After this—I can say my work is over. I'm bored at the house. I'm coming to sew in the Orangery, better to be here than not.

> *(looking at the statue)*

And then, he will keep me Company.

> *(she sits on the bench)*

KING (aside)

Surely, my pretty child, and as long as you like.

PERETTE (working and peeking at the stature from time to time)

They say you look like him—so I'm not astonished if you are pleasing, you are really sweet, you don't know I'm thinking, I'm dreaming only of you and that whenever I get a moment I escape to come see you.

KING (aside)

Now there, at least, is a disinterested love.

PERETTE

Yes, but by peeking at you, I'm not getting on with my work, and someone will notice, and my cousin will scold. Let's go, Mr. His Majesty, don't prevent me from working—without that I'll never come back.

KING (aside)

Indeed—but for the statue.

PERETTE

It's nice to talk with a king, especially when he's not here to answer you.

KING (taking some steps toward her)

I'd really like to—

PERETTE

God! How frightened I'd be if he answered me.

(The king takes a step back and hides behind the statue)

Why, what's going through my head—is it possible, since it is of marble? Come on, now I'm weeping— No, it's over I don't want to remain at Versailles. Sunday I will see this king—if he looks like it the way they say, then I'll come one more time to look at the statue—and then—and then I will leave.

(Perette picks up her basket and is going to withdraw.)

KING (showing himself)

No, Perette—you shan't leave.

PERETTE (letting out a scream)

Ah! ah! my God! How frightened I was—this is the second time I've been startled—I'm not going to dare to raise my eyes.

KING

Why this fright?—isn't it natural that you would want to see the king?

PERETTE (eyes lowered)

Sir—I didn't say—

KING

But as for me, I heard everything!

PERETTE (eyes still lowered)

Since you heard everything, it's not worth the trouble of hiding it from you. Yes, Sir, it's true.

KING

Well, I promise to make you see him, but to do that you must first raise your eyes to me.

PERETTE

Look at you, it's just that I don't dare.

KING

Try anyway—only to know if the statue is a good likeness.

PERETTE (trembling)

What are you saying—you would be—

> (raising her eyes to him and then hiding
> them right away with her hands)

Heavens!

> (Aside)

How he looks like—

KING

Well, Perette—you've seen this king your naive heart loved without knowing him. Know that if his image deserved your tenderness—your charms, you ingenuousness has made an impression on him that will never be erased.

PERETTE

My God! the king saying that to me—to me!

KING

You want to flee—oh! I won't consent to that.

(singing)

Perette, here, tell me—I love you. —Don't be afraid to pledge your word.

TOGETHER

PERETTE

I must tell him that I love him. Truly, it's really an honor for me!

KING

Perette, here tell me—I love you. —Don't be afraid of pledging your faith!

PERETTE

Ah! read in my heart for yourself. Isn't there a love for her king to be seen?

KING

If I have your tenderness
Command as a mistress.
Soon riches
Will be your good fortune.

PERETTE

That's not what I want.
If I am moaning low,
It's only for you, Sire.
I only want your heart.
For my happiness
I only want your heart.

ENSEMBLE

KING

Here, repeat for me: I love you.— Don't be afraid to pledge your faith—

PERETTE

Ah! in my heart read for yourself. Can't you see love for her king?

KING

But it's not merely as a king I want to be loved. It's still more—it's at your knees that I ask it of you.

(The King falls to his knees.)

PERETTE

The king at my knees— God, is it possible? Rather, it's I who ought to ask your pardon for having the audacity to love you without realizing it.

(falling to her knees before him,,hands joined)

Milord, Sire—pardon me, I beg you.

KING (rising)

Yes, I pardon you, charming girl, oh! Yes—get up. Ah! I've never been happier, but someone's coming this way. Perette, don't go far way from the Orangery—we will see each other again today before we separate I intend to give you a souvenir—take this portrait—it's mine—so never lose it.

(The King leaves by the rear.)

PERETTE (trembling)

Your Majesty's portrait. Ah, never, Sire, here's my cousin. My God! what is it I've done there? Heck, it looks like him a lot, too.

(Perette quickly sits down and pretends to sew. Guillaume enters with Grain-d'Orge.)

GRAIN–D'ORGE

I tell you, we will find her here. And, wait—there she is. Announce me, and especially, don't frighten her.

GUILLAUME

Heavens—you are here again, Perette.

PERETTE (still trembling, not raising her eyes)

Well, what! Cousin Guillaume, who's there?

GUILLAUME

I'm bringing someone who wants to see you that I met in Versailles— a baron.

PERETTE

A baron!

GRAIN–D'ORGE

Yes, Grain-d'Orge—the cattle merchant.

PERETTE

You here—has something happened to you—a misfortune perhaps?

GRAIN–D'ORGE

One—it's nothing. Actually two, and they both happened to me to-day.

(sings)

See how much bad luck I have, Miz,
Learning of your departure from the town.
Likewise at court I received the news
That I've just been named baron by the king.
If happiness for us is to be rich,
I am sure that near you wealth won't be lacking.
But when I have ten quarters of nobility,
Damn it, my cattle will be a bit thinner

GUILLAUME

It's true that when I met him he was in a stew! But I told him you were living with me, that you were a gardener at the Orangery, that you could see him and talk to him. Oh, then he jumped on my neck and I thought he was going to choke me.

GRAIN–D'ORGE

Damn! It's quite natural—when a wretch believes he's drowning and he finds a rescue plank—he grabs it.

GUILLAUME

That's it—and you wanted to strangle me—thanks for the preference.

PERETTE

What—you are coming for me?

GRAIN–D'ORGE

Yes, Miz, without knowing if I would find you. Down there dark ideas sometimes came to me—most often they didn't come at all. To the degree that in the midst of my stables—I seemed almost as stupid as my merchandise, getting fatter, getting— but— As for me! Oh! God! you must find me very changed, Perette?

PERETTE

No indeed you are still the same.

GRAIN–D'ORGE

Is she sweet! When I saw that I was taking all this pain to hear, I said to myself Grain-d'Orge you are going to have some unpleasantness you will come to nothing, my lad. Leave for Versailles, you will return to the king what he wants to give you and get back what he wants to take from you. What I came to give back is this bunch of papers, what I want to take back is you, Perette. That's the subject of my trip.

PERETTE

Take me back?

GRAIN–D'ORGE

Yes, Miz.

(sings)

As I am sure of having your heart
I said to myself: let it cost what it costs;
Let's rush to make her happy.
Suddenly, I set out.
At a gallop, I set out.

GUILLAUME

You must be really satisfied, I think. What! baroness! a girl from our town!

PERETTE

It's true, it's really an honor for me, But since this morning, I can't say why, but I'm no longer thinking of marriage.

GRAIN–D'ORGE

That's all the same so long as you return, and from tomorrow, if it pleases you, my millions, my animals and myself, are at your service.

GUILLAUME

Tomorrow, that's going too fast Sir, when you are attached to the service of the king, you must, at least, have his permission to leave it.

PERETTE

Certainly, I can't go far from here.

GRAIN-D'ORGE

It's that, without you, Perette, no nobility, they must give it back to me hand to hand. If not, I will tell them off—I will tell the king himself, I'll say it to everybody.

PERETTE

What, Mr. Grain-d'Orge, you who are so good, you could have evil intentions towards His Majesty?

GRAIN-D'ORGE

Oh! evil intentions, no! But in the end, I'm not a man in service. I have the right to speak at the court. I am a cattle merchant.

GUILLAUME

Ah! my God! now there's His Majesty coming this way—if he heard you—

PERETTE (aside)

Heavens, the King!

GUILLAUME

Quick, Perette, lower your eyes.

GRAIN-D'ORGE

Ah! it's the king. Really this is funny. I didn't think I was brave-

(The King enters with Marsillac, Saint–Aignan, Desmarets and Madame de Montespan.)

KING (to Montespan, giving her his arm)

What, you want to go back by way of the Orangery? Truly, Marquise, I can't conceive why this sudden taste has come to you for strolling in this part of the park.

MADAME DE MONTESPAN

Sire, I don't know—sympathy, perhaps.

KING (low to Marsillac)

Could she have suspicions?

MARSILLAC

I think so and the little one is still there—

MADAME DE MONTESPAN (noticing Perette)

What do I see! oh! the pretty child. I've never seen her at the Orangery.

KING

Prince de Marsillac, make those people withdraw.

(Marsillac takes a step.)

MADAME DE MONTESPAN

Stop, mercy—your subjects are so happy when they can find themselves on the heels of Your Majesty.

GRAIN–D'ORGE (coming forward)

Yes, Sire, which is what decided me to speak to you frankly.

KING

Who is this man?

MARSILLAC

The King asks who you are.

GRAIN–D'ORGE

By Jove, I heard him, I am not deaf.

MADAME DE MONTESPAN (meaningfully)

Perhaps he's the husband or the suitor of this adorable child.

KING (abruptly)

Look, speak, answer. What are you doing there?

GRAIN–D'ORGE

I was coming to speak to you, Sire; Your Majesty doesn't receive me well, but it's all the same. Here's what it is—I am coming from the country, you made me Baron, right? I had accepted at first, because I didn't know how to refuse and because that wouldn't hurt my trade in cattle.

DESMARETS (approaching)

Eh, it's Mr. Grain-d'Orge!

GRAIN–D'ORGE

Just the same—but after they told me this was costing 100,000 crowns, my word!

KING (severely)

Mr. de Grain-d'Orge you must be very well protected to obtain such a favor.

MARSILLAC

What, you will refuse benefits from the king?

GRAIN–D'ORGE

If I don't know how to pay for them, my money, you see, is what I use to buy animals. A baron the more in your court won't do you any good—while a herd the less in mine, that would harm me.

(All the courtiers snicker.)

KING

Silence! Gentlemen I intend those I ennoble to be respected.

GRAIN–D'ORGE (singing)

As regards your order, would you submit to it?
For, if, like you, I am not very submissive,
It's because since my birth I've had wherewithal to buy.
I likewise have the wherewithal to buy good clothes.
While, I confess, grandeur pleases me well enough,
Still, I am chary of paying you for it,
Perhaps you could pay your nobility better
And as for me, I shall better place my money!

KING (smiling)

Meaning, Mr. de Grain-d'Orge, you don't want to reach an agreement with the King of France?

GRAIN–D'ORGE

Indeed, Sire, and if you will allow it, I propose to you that together we make a rough compromise. I agree to pay you for your barony, I ask only for permission to take to the country and marry the one I love right away Little Perette, who's here.

KING (embarrassed)

Ah, it's, it's Perette you want to marry! Why it seems to me that this request—

MADAME DE MONTESPAN (who all this time has had her eyes fixed on those of the king)

—is quite natural, Sire; isn't your greatest privilege that of rendering all your subjects happy? What will it cost you? A word— Let Your Majesty fulfill the wishes of Mr. Grain-d'Orge—he interests me.

(Mute signs of communication between Marsillac and the King.)

GRAIN–D'ORGE

Thanks, Madame.

(aside)

She's a fine woman.

(aloud)

Look, Majesty, what are you going to do? Speak, I wish it! By Jove, for once you will have granted a wish that wasn't that of a Duke or a Peer.

KING

Enough, Mr. de Grain-d'Orge, enough; I am not opposed to this marriage, but only the will of this child can decide it. Come closer, Perette, and make your decision known. He seems to love you. If you love him, also I consent to everything, speak.

GUILLAUME (low to Perette)

Well—what are you thinking? Say quickly that you consent!

GRAIN–D'ORGE

Say it, say it.

PERETTE (timidly approaching the king without looking at him)

(singing)

I owe you gratitude.
You wish the happiness of all your subjects,
But allow me, in your presence,
To dare to speak according to my heart.

Are you agreeing to my prayer?
Perette prefers, such is her will,
To remain a garden girl at court,
Near to you, a gardener,
Than to a be a baroness far from Your Majesty. (repeat)

GUILLAUME (aside)

What did she just say?

GRAIN–D'ORGE

Well—she's refusing me.

MADAME DE MONTESPAN (to Perette)

What are you thinking of my child! Not to want to be the spouse of one the King has just honored with a title, who possesses millions. Sire, try to convince her yourself.

GRAIN–D'ORGE

No, Majesty don't give yourself the trouble over it. Perette's in love with someone else, that's certain. Women have such bizarre ideas. But I know who— Yes, Miz, I understood, I might even say who—

MADAME DE MONTESPAN

Well, speak, my friend; the love of Perette is doubtless pure. Nothing prevents us from knowing it.

KING

Why should we meddle in such details?

GRAIN–D'ORGE

Yes, I could tell it.

KING

It's useless.

GRAIN–D'ORGE

Since you absolutely insist, Sire, I'm going to say it—it's Jean Pierre—there's the cowardly word.

KING (who seems reassured)

Must we contradict the choice of the lovable child?

MADAME DE MONTESPAN

We must work to occupy ourselves in taking care to assure her happiness.

KING

It would truly be vain to make myself pass for a tyrant because a cattle merchant wants to marry a gardener.

(to Perette)

Rest assured, my child, it's not the King who intends to force you to renounce the love you feel.

(shaking her hand, aside)

She seems to me a thousand times prettier!

(aloud)

To the Chateau, gentlemen.

CHORUS

When the great king calls us,
Each one hurries to obey.
One is faithful to his orders
And duty is a pleasure. (repeat)

> *(The King Leaves, followed by all the persons in his suite except Saint–Aignan and Marsillac.)*

GRAIN–D'ORGE

Ah! that's the way he protects me, the King! Ah, that's how he treats his nobles! Well, I no longer want his barony—let him arrange about it with someone else.

MARSILLAC

One moment, Mr. de Grain-d'Orge—the King never takes back what he has given.

GRAIN–D'ORGE

Ah, you call that giving, you! We'll see about that! I'm Normand—I'd rather go to law, or if I lose, then I will speak for my money, I—I will say whatever I wish I will do what pleases me, I will go above you, I will stroll everywhere you do, I will have myself carried in arm chairs, I will purchase footstools, ah, ah, I am going to give you some of myself.

SAINT-AIGNAN

Certainly, you will have that right, Mr. de Grain-d'Orge.

MARSILLAC

Will Baron de Grain-d'Orge do me the honor of accepting my arm?

SAINT-AIGNAN

I want to show you all the marvels of Versailles, Mr. de Grain-d'Orge.

MARSILLAC

I pretend to the honor to take you to the treasury, Mr. Baron de Grain-d'Orge.

GRAIN-D'ORGE (taking their arms impatiently)

That's it, escort me everywhere; I want to have the approval of the Court, I do. I want favors I want honors, I must have 'em for a hundred thousand crowns.

(they leave dragging him away)

Goodbye, Gardener-girl!

GUILLAUME (to Perette)

Let's go, come with us, now, cousin. Since you don't want to be a baroness, return to your work.

MADAME DE MONTESPAN (appearing)

Stay, Perette. I need to speak to you.

PERETTE

To me, Madame?

GUILLAUME

That suffices, I'll withdraw all by myself.

(aside)

Sonofabitch! what's this all about? If the court descends to the garden, the garden will rise to the court. I see myself at least as Vicomte of Orange, so I do.

(he leaves)

MADAME DE MONTESPAN

Approach, my child.

PERETTE

I await your order, Madame.

MADAME DE MONTESPAN

My orders! I have only a prayer to address to you. Your age, your sweetness, all inspire an interest in you which one doesn't know how to defend against. I try to deserve your confidence, your friendship.

PERETTE

You won't talk to me any further about marrying Mr. Grain-d'Orge?

MADAME DE MONTESPAN

I only want to speak of him—the one who loves you and that you love and if it's possible for me to contribute to your happiness.

PERETTE

Oh, no, Madame, for I no longer have anything to deSire.

MADAME DE MONTESPAN (worried)

What? What do you mean?

PERETTE

Nothing, except that the one I love has learned of it without getting angry. That's all that I could ask.

MADAME DE MONTESPAN

And you've dared to form the hope?

PERETTE

Oh, I hope for nothing except to see him from time to time and to think of him always.

MADAME DE MONTESPAN

But if I had enough power to convince the King to give you for a husband—the one you love.

PERETTE

That's impossible, Madame, he's married.

MADAME DE MONTESPAN

Married! poor child and was he able to make you a confession of a passion that his duty forbids him to publish aloud? Doubtless it's one of the gentleman of His Majesty who, taking their master for a model, ceaselessly offer to one or another the homage of a love they don't feel.

PERETTE (excitedly)

What! Madam—you think that the King—

MADAME DE MONTESPAN (aside)

It's him!

(aloud)

Alas, my child, he's always caused nothing but tears to those who had the weakness of loving him—you don't know all that this love could cost you in remorse! For your happiness, for mine, it's necessary to triumph over it.

PERETTE

For your happiness,—then you love him, too?

MADAME DE MONTESPAN (meaningfully)

Who—the King?

PERETTE (worried and lowering her eyes, aside)

What have I said?

MADAME DE MONTESPAN

Yes, Perette—powerful bonds attach me to him!

PERETTE (aside)

What an idea! if she was—

(aloud)

Ah! Madame, if you are the Queen, pardon me.

(Perette falls at the feet of Madame de Montespan.)

MADAME DE MONTESPAN (raising her)

Stand up! No question, the king has made brilliant promises to you. To enrich you is easy, but to grant you a true, lasting love, that's what he can never do.

PERETTE (upset)

Oh! I don't wish anything, Madame!

MADAME DE MONTESPAN

Listen, my child! Can you have heard the name of the Duchess de la Valliere spoken of?

PERETTE

They spoke to me of her as the most beautiful lady of the court!

MADAME DE MONTESPAN

Meaning that she was loved by the king. Well! This La Valliere who sacrificed her reputation to Louis XIV was the butt of the just wrath of an offended queen—after two years, not of happiness, but of scandalous notoriety, was forced to enshroud her shame in the depths of a convent, imploring vainly a souvenir from the one who loved her—as he would never be capable of loving you—

PERETTE

And he completely forgot her!

MADAME DE MONTESPAN

Since that time he's never mentioned her name, and when, as today, the Duchess addresses him and reproaches him for her abandonment, he doesn't deign even to cast a glance at her letters—read yourself. This was sent to Versailles yesterday from the Carmelites!

PERETTE (taking the letter hesitantly)

What, Madame, you want—

MADAME DE MONTESPAN

Read it, it's necessary.

PERETTE (reading)

Sire, it's not for me that I implore your pity, but for my daughter, for your child who has no one to sustain her on earth except you. Take care of our poor Louise—if you must never think of her mother—another has succeeded me in your heart—to the Marquise de Montespan, another.

MADAME DE MONTESPAN

Keep going, keep going!

PERETTE

To the Marquise de Montespan, another will succeed without doubt. Already the rumor is spreading at the court that you have given her a rival. How can I, from the depths of this retreat, make my voice heard to the one who would be unfortunate enough to love you like me!

(with the greatest emotion)

I would tell her to flee you, for the love of a king leaves only tears after it, only regrets. What you inspire is a hundred times more cruel than death.

MADAME DE MONTESPAN

Well, Perette what will you do?

PERETTE

From tomorrow I will leave—I will finish forever.

MADAME DE MONTESPAN

Believe that my benefits will follow you everywhere.

PERETTE

I told you, Madame, I want nothing—nothing except Your Majesty's pardon.

MADAME DE MONTESPAN

Heavens! here's the king! Leave, leave quickly.

PERETTE (she heads towards the back, stops and says to herself, weeping)

No, I will never see him again.

KING (entering without seeing the Marquise and stopping Perette)

Well, where are you running to this way, my pretty child?

PERETTE

Sire! The Queen! The Queen!

(Perette escapes. The King remains stupefied, the Marquise looks at him, smiling ironically.)

KING

What's she mean? The Marquise!

(aloud)

I was looking for you, Madam—

MADAME DE MONTESPAN (trying to seem calm)

Sire, permit me to congratulate you on the beauty of your new protégé and the nobility of your tastes.

KING

What—you imagine!

MADAME DE MONTESPAN

So modest. Ah! Your Majesty has made more difficult conquests.

KING

My royalty often does more than my person.

MADAME DE MONTESPAN

At least, Your Majesty doesn't fear to admit them—but it is one whose rank—

KING

Are you forgetting that the King of France raises all who approach him? Titles, honors, isn't it my will that disposes of them?

MADAME DE MONTESPAN

Pardon, Sire to have dared before you—

KING

Come, come, marquise, I admit this meeting here must give you some umbrage, one would swear that I was coming to a rendezvous.

MADAME DE MONTESPAN

Indeed, but appearances are so deceiving.

KING

Yes, especially when one is like me.

MADAME DE MONTESPAN

Incapable of betraying sworn faith-faithful to his love.

KING

My love! Would you like a proof of it, speak I'm making you a Duchess.

MADAME DE MONTESPAN

A new title for me! Ah! that's not gallant, Sire, you are treating me like a disgraced minister.

KING

Then what can I do to prove to you—

MADAME DE MONTESPAN

Nothing, because I know everything—that young girl, you love her.

KING

Who told you that?

MADAME DE MONTESPAN

She herself.

KING

Well! isn't it the duty of a good king to have affection for all his subjects?

MADAME DE MONTESPAN

And even the female ones?

KING (taking the hand of the Marquise)

When one has no love except for one alone.

(He kisses her hand.)

MADAME DE MONTESPAN

Except for one alone. Wait, there yet remains a way for you to make me believe in your tenderness.

KING

Speak, I don't want to refuse anything to you—what is it?

MADAME DE MONTESPAN

It's to offer me, this very day, in the presence of your courtiers, what has already distanced itself from me—the pretty portrait of Your Majesty, painted by Mignard and so boasted by all the court. Well, you aren't answering?

KING

Wait, Marquise, ask of me anything else.

MADAME DE MONTESPAN

It's disposed of already—I understand, a rival happier than me—

KING

No, Madame it's for—it's for the Queen!

MADAME DE MONTESPAN

For the Queen?

KING

Do you still doubt?

MADAME DE MONTESPAN

Doubt? Ah! You Majesty manages so well.

(Enter Guillaume with Perette.)

GUILLAUME

Come on, come this way, I tell you we will find someone to speak to. Since you tell me you found this portrait, it must be returned.

KING (aside)

The little one again!

(to the Marquise)

Come, Madam.

GUILLAUME (with embarrassment)

Excuse, Sire, if I dare to disturb You—it's, that having seen in the hands of this child, the portrait of Your Majesty—

KING (aside)

Ah! the clumsy!

MADAME DE MONTESPAN

The portrait of the King?

PERETTE

Pardon me, Sire! if this portrait is found in my hands.

(sings)

Just now, near the Orangery,
You left it by error.
I found your cherished image

And I hid it in my heart.
A single instant I dared to pretend
To keep it; it must be agreed.
But now, I must return it,
For it no longer belongs to me.

MADAME DE MONTESPAN (meaningfully, and watching the king)

That portrait was for the Queen?

PERETTE (presenting it to her ingenuously)

Take it back, then, Madam!

GUILLAUME (tugging her skirt)

Well! what is it you are doing there?

PERETTE (low to Guillaume)

Then she's not the Queen?

GUILLAUME (embarrassed)

Huh! why, yes—almost. She's Madame De Montespan.

PERETTE (aside)

How mistaken I was!

(Enter Marsillac, Desmarets, Saint–Aignan, Grain-d'Orge and other gentlemen, etc.)

GRAIN–D'ORGE (ridiculously dressed and surrounded by gentlemen)

Let me be announced, let me be greeted! Beware when I pass. I am satisfied with you, gentlemen, my colleagues, you are very likable and your Sherry wine, too.

DESMARETS

Silence before the King! Your Majesty, permit me to present to him—

KING

The Baron de Grain-d'Orge.

GRAIN–D'ORGE

Better than that, Sire! Since I paid cash, they named me Count. They made me a good deal!

GUILLAUME

What, cousin, you are going to be a Countess?

GRAIN–D'ORGE

Countess—Will she consent now?

GUILLAUME

Pardon—it's that, before His Majesty, I don't dare repeat what Perette just told me.

KING

Speak.

MADAME DE MONTESPAN

The king allows it.

GUILLAUME

Ah! then I can tell you that just now I treated this poor child so roughly because I saw her weep without knowing why. Cousin, she said to me in her little voice which goes like this: I was wrong, he's a fine man, Mr. Grain-d'Orge, he would be incapable of deceiving a poor girl, him! so, if he still wanted me! well, I will be his wife.

GRAIN–D'ORGE

She said that? What, does she love me? She loves me, perhaps?

PERETTE

No, cousin, I don't want them to say, now that Mr. Grain d'Orge is a great lord!

GRAIN–D'ORGE

Oh! yes, if it's only that, don't let it bother you, Perette. If my title papers for count offend you I will lock 'em in a drawer. I won't go wearing my nobility in my buttonhole—not so stupid.

MADAME DE MONTESPAN

You are going to leave, Perette. Be happy, that's the wish of the King, and my wish, too.

KING (spitefully)

Doubtlessly—I'll keep it infinitely.

(to Grain-d'Orge and casting a glance at Perette)

Mr. de Grain-d'Orge, I permit you to present your wife to the court, I intend to receive the Countess.

PERETTE

May Your Majesty pardon me, but now I will never leave the country.

GRAIN−D'ORGE (strutting)

Oh, don't worry, I will come to see you all alone. That will come to same thing.

KING

Gentlemen, the hour of Council is here.

(low to Perette)

Perette—au revoir!

(offering Madame de Montespan his hand)

You see plainly, Marquise, that you alarmed yourself wrongly.

(Low to Marsillac, slipping the portrait into his hand)

Tomorrow this portrait to the widow Scarron.

(aloud)

Let's leave!

CHORUS (the king leaves with his court during this chorus)

Let's sing the glory of this great king.
He's just fulfilled all our wishes.
One day history will say
Louis has made everybody happy.

CURTAIN

www.ingramcontent.com/pod-product-compliance
Lightning Source LLC
Chambersburg PA
CBHW021121020426

42331CB00004B/570